Contents

1
PERSONAL DEVELOPMENT

PERSONAL DEVELOPMENT

One of the most important aspects of improving the customer experience is to consider your individual performance. It seems like human nature that we often seek to find fault with or blame others before really considering our personal levels of expertise and execution.

Many people believe that they know and understand good service. They probably aren't incorrect. We've been taught and have heard about customer service since we were children; however, having and using our knowledge and expertise are two very different things.

It won't be hard to find agreement with your knowledge, but the truth about your individual performance may be a little different from what you expect.

Personal development with customer service may be one of the best moves you can make with your career. As with emotional intelligence, empathy, and other soft skills, those who deliver exceptional customer service will be more sought after professionally when compared to those who demonstrate poor skills in these areas.

It is fitting to start this book with a chapter on personal development because what we say, do, and think will have a significant impact on not only our own performance but also the performance of others.

If you've read this far, don't quickly discount this chapter as not for you but for everyone else. Ask yourself the tough questions. One of the toughest and hardest to answer may be "What are my customer-service habits, and how well do I deliver customer excellence?" This of course is appropriate for both the internal and external aspects of customer-service techniques.

Remember, for now it is not about considering what you know; it is about considering how you execute or practice what you know.

CUSTOMER NEEDS—UNDERSTAND THEM OR WISH THAT YOU HAD

Knowing exactly what customers want may be better stated as "I think I know exactly what they want." Fast, friendly, and courteous are all things that are synonymous with exceptional customer service, but understanding customer needs may not always be so simple.

Have you ever had a conversation with someone who insists on finishing your sentences? I know I have, and I know I've been the one finishing the sentence for others from time to time.

Usually it isn't so much that we believe we know it all; it is probably more about demonstrating that we are on the same page. At least that may be what we tell ourselves.

Riding a bike, lifting some weights, running, jogging, or walking, exercise takes energy. The same is true for being a great listener, having extreme concentration, and even reading a book.

Do you work hard to understand your customers' needs?

Understanding Customer Needs

If you're going to understand your customers, you're going to have to listen, and therefore you're going to have to work hard to understand. Finishing their sentences may signal that you're on the same page, or it may signal that you don't have time to listen.

If you're going to understand what the customer wants or needs, you should consider doing more of this:

1. **Making time.** Being hurried seldom helps. Signal that you have the time or will make the time.

2. **Arriving.** Sometimes it doesn't matter if you are first or last; what will matter the most is that you arrive, mentally and sometimes physically.

3. **Being patient.** Not everyone wears his or her emotions or thoughts on his or her sleeves. Allow for expressions of pain points. Practice *patience*.

4. **Assuming nothing.** Thinking you know the immediate answer to their problems sometimes works; it also sometimes doesn't. Assume less often.

5. **Having no anger.** Anger never helps. Passion is good, but getting emotional probably isn't going to help you learn more about their needs.

Engage with your customers, do the math, and get on the same page. Use your energy, because understanding customer needs isn't always about a race, nor is it necessarily about being first. In addition, it's almost never about being rushed or hurried.

Sometimes trying to be first just may make you last or, in the eyes of the customer, seem to not exist at all.

THREE CUSTOMER SERVICE HABITS YOU CAN CHANGE RIGHT NOW

The concept of replacing bad habits with good habits is nothing new. It works for things like eating, exercising, and even sleeping. Many people have a customer-service obligation at work even though they may not always realize it. Which customer-service habits can you change right now?

Regardless of your workplace role, chances are good that you can improve teamwork, make others' jobs and lives easier, and make your organization more efficient and profitable with a few simple habits.

Customer Service Habits

Here are three easy ones:

- **Assuming needs.** Priding yourself on knowing exactly what the customer wants can make both you and the customer feel pretty good. Getting it wrong can be painful and costly. Ask more questions, listen better, and give the customer an opportunity to discuss what the result should look like. Assume less, and inquire more.

- **Meeting needs.** Many people are conditioned for finishing the task. It seems that sometimes we lose sight of why we are doing the task and instead only focus on finishing it. Finishing is important, but we need to be sure we are meeting the needs of those involved. Sometimes having patience and spending time are just as important as finishing.

- **Opening doors.** You should leave the door open for future opportunities. How you close a conversation or a transaction often has something to do with when you'll get the next opportunity. You want to ensure that the door is open. Consider that "have a nice day" is different from "see you tomorrow."

Change Habits Now

It's easy for even the most business-minded people to slip into bad habits. We're often a product of how we subconsciously move about during our day.

Customer-service habits are for everyone. Treat every interaction and opportunity with the intention to help.

You know what to do. Replace worn-out habits with fresh ones.

BOOST YOUR CAREER WITH CUSTOMER SERVICE SKILLS

There is considerable chatter about differences across the workforce generations (see appendix A for workforce generations descriptions). Many consider respect as problematic, with any generational representation different from your own as lacking it. Traditionals and baby boomers believe that millennials and gen Z lack respect for their elders and vice versa. We also can't forget about gen X; they are in the mix too.

Some people also connect respect with customer service. It is common for earlier generations to believe that the more recent generations lack manners and respect in service transactions. Regardless of your generation, one way to boost your career is with customer-service mastery.

Many people believe that they know the art of exceptional customer service. No doubt customer-service skills are not hard to know or understand. The real challenge with customer service is more about culture, habits, and traditions. Knowing the basics is commonplace; practicing what you know is often a different story. Individual performance stimulates role modeling; role modeling stimulates groups; and groups and departments, along with organizational leadership, define cultural norms. The best performing individuals and organizations practice what they preach.

Boost Your Career

Do you want to boost your career? Do you really, really want to boost your career? One of the best social skills you can master is being a leader in delivering exceptional customer service.

It is simple, and here are three steps to consider:

1. Ask yourself, "How can I give more to this situation?" You need to be thinking of things like ease of use, value, or even general kindness. Having good manners, being respectful, and demonstrating that you care will go a long way.

2. Focus on needs. You have to discover the needs of the person or organization. You do this by asking questions and being an exceptional listener. Then your goal is to make your delivery exceptional and memorable—so much so that they will want more.

3. Replicate. Everyone knows that practice makes perfect. Remember that the concept of customer service is easy. Having exceptional habits of customer service is typically more difficult. Learn and understand the basics. Practice them every time. Make them become habits.

If customer service is so simple, why is there so much turmoil around its delivery? The answer is also simple. Customer service requires thought, action, and a set of behaviors to develop as habits. Many people forget their roles or are not engaged enough to care.

Customer Service Mastery

If you want to boost your career, master the concepts and deliver exceptional customer service—not just on the job but everywhere.

It is for all generations.

WHEN NO PROBLEM IS A PROBLEM

We probably experience many customer-service interactions every day, not just at the convenience store, on the telephone, or in our workplaces but everywhere. Do you recognize that when you say, "No problem," it may actually be a problem?

Psychologically when someone says, "No problem," it may be interpreted as a form of sarcasm. Consciously or subconsciously, the customer listens and reacts based on hearing the word "problem."

We learn about customer service at a very young age. Nearly everyone understands the importance of a smile, a friendly greeting, and making a difference for someone else. What are your practices though? Do you have the right habits?

No Biggie

When I was a teenager, I remember a popular phrase. It was used so often that I'm not sure its true meaning was really understood. After everything that happened—every time there was something going on that required a follow-up response—we might have heard "no biggie."

People said, "No biggie" all the time. I guess it meant not to worry, no offense taken, or maybe sometimes it meant you're welcome. "No biggie," just like, "no problem," may invite an unfavorable reaction for the customer; while it is unintentional, be aware that words might alter the mood of any interaction.

Sometimes our habits are not just actions. They may also be words or phrases. Habits may include a thoughtless response of jargon that we apply to more than one situation.

No Problem

In customer-service scenarios, we may want to consider that the commonly used phrase "no problem" may actually be a problem.

Consider some of these scenarios:

- No problem. I'll call you as soon as I find out more information.

- If you have any trouble, just call me—no problem.

- We can fix that, no problem.

Have you ever considered that sometimes when we say, "No problem," the customers may feel that there actually was a problem? All of us may be psychologically connected to words through past experiences and the images that we form as we listen—on the surface it may sound like we are being nice, and everything is OK. However, the customer may wonder if it really is a problem after all.

Perhaps their interaction interrupted your other work. They may feel like they were asking for something special that was an inconvenience to you.

Worse yet, they may decide consciously or subconsciously that they don't want to be a problem in the future.

You're Welcome

Perhaps "no problem" is misunderstood. Maybe we should change that habit. We could just as easily say, "You're welcome."

CONFUSED ABOUT THE CUSTOMER AND SURVIVING THE STORM

"Know your customers." That is just one phrase of many that may relate to the worth of understanding more about your customers. Have you ever been confused about the customer?

Blockbuster might have been confused because if they really knew and wanted to be a top player, they might have looked more closely at streaming video before they lost so much of their market share. Eventually Blockbuster[1] filed for bankruptcy; and after a short time under bankruptcy protection, Dish Network purchased what remained. Dish still owns and operates using the Blockbuster brand in some streaming on-demand markets. I am not sure any segment or representation of the brand will survive what Blockbuster may have once considered a digital storm.

Educational systems, whether it is public schools or colleges and universities, may want to work hard on understanding the customers and their products. Otherwise, their customers may continue to move away from what has been a long-standing tradition of brick-and-mortar institutions. Forget where you came from, your true purpose, or the reason for the customer, and the customer may forget about you. Emerging technologies may be a storm, and storms sometimes change traditions.

Brick-and-mortar retailers, luxury goods, and traditional advertising agencies are also among those who have a lot to consider. The storm is hitting them too. It's likely that only a few are exempt, and that exemption is temporary.

Reality Is Tough

One thing is certain: most things aren't staying the same. For good or for bad, things are constantly changing. Name an industry, and name the traditional giants of that industry; if they haven't substantially changed, they are probably diminishing in size.

Many industry leaders claim allegiance to doing everything possible to better serve their customers, but few of them get it right. Sometimes they get it right in the C suite, but they fail to create the right culture. The opposite is true too. Sometimes businesses get it right in the trenches only to hit roadblocks in the C suite. (See appendix B for five tips on communicating with the C suite.)

Confused about the Customer

Here are a few questions to ask yourself to avoid being confused about the customer:

- What are we doing that punishes the customer?
- Who is defining our product, and what is it?
- What makes our product valuable?
- Are we listening to the customer, and how?
- How are we measuring customer satisfaction?

Perhaps there isn't a perfect answer to any of those, but honest assessment of these and many more questions is critical for success. I promise you that most who read those five questions believe they are already beyond them. I wonder what their customers would say.

Surviving the Storm

Customer service isn't just a department, and neither is sales. Businesses that lack an understanding of a customer service and sales culture are businesses that won't survive the storm.

Those who understand…well, they are the storm.

CUSTOMER EXPECTATIONS AND TOP PERFORMERS

Being deeply connected with the customer experience is much more than identifying that you'll take care of the customer. Often forgotten or easily misunderstood is that customer expectations are set by everyone they interact with, not just you or your organization.

Customer Expectations

When you are accustomed to being asked, "Did you save room for dessert?" you may not order if you aren't asked. When your packages arrive in two days or less, anything longer may be too long. Experiences set customer expectations. It is not a slogan, tag line, or your mission statement.

The same is true internally in organizations. The boss or the departments that you serve will base every interaction on the best experiences they have had. If they have had excellence before you, the bar may be set high.

Opportunities to Perform

Some may suggest that customers are trainable. The quality, speed, and value that they receive repeatedly will likely become their expectations. They learn what to expect, when, and how.

The organization that follows through, is appropriately fast, and provides the greatest value may also be the one that customers compare with everyone else.

Your performance in your job role may also be held to a similar comparison against other top performers.

What this really means is that every interaction, every touch point, is an opportunity—one that will be measured against what the customer expects. Any person or organization that sets the bar higher may become the one to beat.

Best Performance

Your customer service is not as good as what you say it is. It is only as good as what the customer expects.

YOUR CUSTOMER SERVICE IS NOT AS GOOD AS WHAT YOU SAY IT IS. IT IS ONLY AS GOOD AS WHAT THE CUSTOMER EXPECTS.

In a world of fast-paced, technology-driven performance, the best scenario may be having to meet or exceed your previous best performance. Otherwise, you'll have to live with the expectation set by someone else.

THREE REASONS TO MAKE CUSTOMER SERVICE BETTER

Everyone is a critic. People are often critical about customer service when they are expecting to receive. What if everyone worked to make customer service better?

One of my professional speaking colleagues has a slogan: "Because we can!" Jeffrey Hayzlett[2] is a professional speaking rock star, and I love his slogan. While I believe that the intent of Jeffrey's slogan is to be motivational and inspirational regarding hard work, determination, and relentless pursuit, it may be applicable in other ways too.

Make Customer Service Better

Should our personal and professional interactions with other people have more customer service flair? Can we make customer service better? Sometimes I think so, and other times I know so.

Here are three great reasons why we should:

1. **Fairness.** Sometimes it just seems like life isn't fair. If we can help balance the scale, right the wrongs, and turn things around, why shouldn't we? An even better question might be: Why wouldn't we? If there is a shortcoming, make it better. Make it fair.

2. **Generosity.** Certainly, the bottom line is important, and any business transaction should be two-way, not just one. Can your offer be more generous? Will generosity cause more reciprocation? In a world that would benefit from improved customer service, I think being more generous is part of the process.

3. **Respect.** It seems that recently there is a lot of chatter about respect: respect across the generations, respect in political circles, and certainly respect toward our customers. Time, value, and money are all important, and let's not forget that we should deliver with the utmost respect.

Because We Can

In business, we often size up the competition to see what they are doing. We consider their offers, values, and prices. Competition may drive us to do things because we feel that we have to. What if we did it for a different reason? Imagine if we changed the philosophy.

Should we make customer service better?

I think yes *because we can!*

WHY DIGITAL CUSTOMER SERVICE IS FOR YOU

You are in a new race: the race for digital excellence. Don't be alarmed; be happy. Digital customer service is happening for us, not to us.

Things are always changing. We can argue for good, bad, or somewhere in between. Change often makes people feel uneasy, nervous, and afraid. From generation to generation, things are changing.

Generational Differences

Generational shifts happen for a combination of reasons. In our modern history, we can attribute these shifts to some combination of three factors (see appendix C, generational definition trap): major socioeconomic shifts, technology, and times of war.

You can clearly see the shifting and weaving of these patterns when you consider the five generations we currently have active in our workforce.

What changes are affecting customer service? One of the biggest may be the digital revolution.

Digital isn't new, but the rapid rate of implementation is causing a significant shift. Things are going digital. How will digital impact you?

Digital Customer Service

When it comes to customer service, here are three of many areas to consider:

1. **Security.** You go through a fingerprint reader at Epcot, and your boarding pass for airline travel is a QR code on your telephone. The face of security is changing. Not only are video-surveillance cameras installed in many public places, but they are also improving the customer experience with speed, safety, and comfort.

2. **World of Mouth.** Sales and customer-service experts know both the benefits and dangers of word of mouth. Today we have to face the risks and rewards of world of mouth with social media. Accept it or deny it, social-media data impact

revenues and success. Ignore it, and get left behind.

3. **Access to Choices.** Do you want to engage tech-savvy customers and especially those representing the millennial and Gen Z populations? Start thinking more about mobile technologies, smartphones, and downloadable apps. Fast, easy, and with better features—this is the future of customer service.

Going Digital

Most of all, remember that change is happening all around us. As a result, if you want the best customer experience, you may have to think more digitally. Consider your choices, be innovative, and always consider your target market.

It is all happening *for you*.

CHAPTER 1—SUMMARY

Personal or professional development is often about choice. Many people believe that years of experience will be the best predictor of future success. Certainly, experience matters, but what may matter the most is preparedness.

Preparedness means that you equip yourself with the knowledge and skills that are necessary to deliver. Competence proves that you can. If you have read this far, you may already be a step ahead of the pack.

Today, more often, I find people who want the position, want the bigger paycheck, yet they are unwilling to read, study, or become better prepared. They lack competence, and it is often noticeable, not always during self-reflection, but it is often very visible to those looking on.

Therefore, personal development is strongly connected to choice. People choose to read, study, or continue their education. They choose to gain experience, gain knowledge, and become more competent. Some may believe that it just happens, and some educational experiences are like that. Those excelling at their careers are likely doing something to purposely improve them.

Developing a personal or organizational culture with a focus on customer service is also about choice.

2
MANAGEMENT

MANAGEMENT

Being responsible for a team or an entire organization isn't an easy task. Effectively managing customer-service policies and procedures may on the surface sound relatively easy. It is not.

Often one of the biggest disconnects I encounter when working with organizations is a difference between what members of management say and their intentions when compared to what employees hear and the actions they then take.

A few years ago, I worked with a small business, helping them advance their positioning with building a customer-service culture. We had several campfire-type discussions. (A campfire discussion means sitting in a large circular group with a facilitated conversation.) During these conversations, it quickly became clear that there was a difference between management expectations and what was happening on the front line.

Business owners or managers may hold meeting where they talk about the bottom line, avoiding waste, and maintaining as much profit margin as possible. This is a good idea. However, what is sometimes heard by the front line is that "times are tough, we're not making it. And if we don't watch every penny, someone will lose his or her job."

As a reaction to hearing this, albeit incorrectly, the front line starts doing things that punish the customer. They hold back on the little thrills. They stop focusing on making the moment memorable. Their focus becomes saving and preserving every penny.

In one case that I recall, a customer needed a bolt and another small item to touch up something on the product he just purchased. This was a big purchase, exceeding $20,000. The front-line person suggested that he would contact the manufacturer and submit this claim as a warranty repair.

In the front-line person's mind, he was being courteous and doing the right thing. Why should the company pay for this when the manufacturer made the mistake? Good point—but good points don't always make smart choices in customer service.

WHY SHOULD THE COMPANY PAY FOR THIS WHEN THE
MANUFACTURER MADE THE MISTAKE?

The fix for this situation was less than ten dollars. When those in top management heard this story, they were taken aback. In their minds, they couldn't understand why the front line didn't solve this for the customer immediately. The front-line person felt that he was merely protecting the bottom line. Alas, there was a difference between what was said and what was heard.

Managing customer service and creating an exceptional customer experience every time require extra effort and special care.

WHO IS THE VOICE OF YOUR BUSINESS?

Who is the voice of your business? In a word, everyone.

Many businesses probably feel pretty good about managing their inbound sales calls. They probably have a great website and probably have well-established sales professionals managing all their web-based sales as well as those old-school sales that come in from callers.

What about all the other departments or employees in your business that might interact with the outside world? Do they need to know how to manage calls and perhaps be well trained in customer-service techniques?

I don't do a lot of cold calling, but I do some. Most weeks I have a specific target for the number of new potential clients I'm trying to reach. I'm not alone; many businesspeople and entrepreneurs are out there trying to build better relationships and earn more business, and a lot of them establish and build these relationships on the telephone or with video technology.

In today's world, many calls end up in a voice-mail message, but occasionally you'll get to speak with a real live person. Sometimes it may be the person who you were trying to reach, and sometimes it might be someone far removed from your target.

What Is the Point?

The point I'm about to make is that every autoattendant, voice-mail system, or person gives you an impression of that business. Every button you have to push, the length of time you spend listening to a recorded message, or the tone or perceived attitude of each recorded personal greeting is telling you something about that business.

On a recent call, I reached someone in a department who was close to my target but not an exact match. My impression was not good. The person listened patiently and gave me a few seconds to introduce the reason for my call; she didn't seem especially hurried or annoyed, but when it came time to help me reach my intended target, she acted like I just asked for the social-security numbers and birth dates of her entire team.

I'm typically not a suspicious person, but my suspicion in this case is that she has been the victim of an internal assault for giving out anyone's name or identifying anyone in a specific position. My asking to get to a specific person in a specific job role terrified her.

What Is the Message?

The message here is that your business has people who are outside of your inbound fielding team (or sales group) who may receive some occasional inbound calls from a potential vendor or a misrouted customer, and those people who are representing your business are creating a first impression. They are the voice of your business. They represent everything that your business is and everything that your business does, including how it respects people and other businesses.

THEY REPRESENT EVERYTHING THAT YOUR BUSINESS IS AND EVERYTHING THAT YOUR BUSINESS DOES, INCLUDING HOW IT RESPECTS PEOPLE AND OTHER BUSINESSES.

It doesn't matter how awesome your website, marketing materials, or television ads are; when someone touches your operation through a telephone call, he or she is visualizing every moment of that interaction as a representation of your business.

The worst part of this is that everyone gets it—this isn't rocket science—yet so many businesses fail to manage this properly. Often their thought is, *We've got better things to do.*

What to Do?

If you're considering making a difference for your business, you'll need to review your autoattendant answering system, and you'll need to consider who may be receiving calls. Many businesses have what is referred to as a dial-by-name directory, and these are great, but then an outside caller may reach anyone in that system.

What does each employee have recorded as his or her personal greeting message? How does it sound? How often is it changed or updated? What is the protocol for managing an inbound call? What are the guidelines? Do you have a response-time policy? Are their voices clear, warm, and friendly?

Does *every* employee know and understand?

So I have to ask. Who is the voice of your business?

Everyone.

CUSTOMER SERVICE BREAKDOWN OR WEAR DOWN

We probably all have a bad customer-service story. In fact, when it comes to customer experiences, it is what most people talk about: the bad stuff, the horror story. It's what people tell their families, friends, and next-door neighbors.

I've heard a lot of bad customer-service stories. During many of my customer-service seminars, I typically have at least one activity that draws focus to the participants' positive experiences, specifically to get them thinking about what a good experience feels like, rather than creating a focus on what is wrong or broken.

Breakdown

Some organizations will self-identify when they have a problem with their customer-service policy or procedures. They are constantly striving for feedback, they listen well, and they find effective ways to survey their customer base; they even monitor social-media channels.

They'll often go to great lengths, and it pays off because it helps them quickly identify things that are broken: a bad policy, a mishandled transaction, a quality issue, or they may even catch a negative online post or unfavorable comparison with their competition.

We may hear some of these complaints:

"My French fries were cold."

"The doctor ordered the wrong test."

"The landscaper killed the grass."

"They sent me the wrong product."

Resolving or fixing breakdowns in the customer experience is sometimes costly but is easily identified.

All of this is great, but so often this is only identifying the breakdown in customer service or quality. Is there something else? Absolutely—and that something else is often about wear down.

Wear Down

What happens when an organization finds a gap or hole in a policy or procedure? It creates an addendum to the rules.

What happens to a rule that is applied over and over again across long periods of time? It often loses some of its purpose or integrity. It may fade, or it weakens.

The question may become, "Do we take back a broken product beyond its warranty period?" The answer is often yes, and this likely makes sense, but over time, the CSR (customer-service representative) may completely forget about the warranty period.

What often is not so easily identified is how the rules change over time. This may not be so much about a breakdown in policy or procedure but more representative of a wearing down. It's when the intent of a policy or procedure becomes more nebulous over time.

"I drove my car one hundred and fifty thousand miles, but it had excellent care, and now the motor is fading. I want it fixed for free."

"My house roof is thirty-five years old but just sprung a leak. I'm calling the roofer to complain."

"I've had my smartphone for three years and religiously charged it in the proper manner, but the battery is fading, and I want a replacement."

What would the CSR or the organization do to solve any of these problems? Provide a new car, a new roof, or a brand-new smartphone? I'm dramatizing for illustration purposes, but a bend in the rules over time can become costly.

Wear Down Works Both Ways

The opposite can also be true. What happens or how do you identify when a CSR or another organization representative inadvertently tightens the rules? This is also wear down—a wear down of the intent of the guidelines, policies, or procedures.

The best organizations don't just fix breakdowns; they are also monitoring for and adjusting to wear downs.

Do you know of anything that is wearing down?

FIVE MANAGEMENT ACTIONS THAT PUNISH THE CUSTOMER

Have you experienced management decisions or policies that punish the customer? Building a brand isn't always easy, and we know that finding new customers is harder and more expensive than maintaining existing ones.

Unfortunately, sometimes organizations or brands with great potential make disappointing choices. Too often policies or procedures aren't designed to help the customer; they are designed to protect the business. Great brands have figured out how to balance both.

Don't Punish the Customer

Here are a few management decisions or behaviors that may be hurting much more than helping.

1. **Taking a chance that it will be OK.** This is the decision to release a product or service that is noticeably flawed in the hope that maybe the customer won't notice or complain. Some customers will say little or nothing. They will just go away quietly.

2. **Believing that the customer has wrongful intentions.** Certainly, there are some customers who have unfair intentions; however, too many rules to fight the few with wrongful intent may send a signal of mistrust to those who are loyal. Loyalty goes both ways.

3. **Insisting that policy is never broken or adjusted.** A policy or warranty that is never adjusted may be the first signal that a divorce is coming. A reasonable decision to resolve is better than a strong position to do nothing.

4. **Believing that questions waste time.** If you are answering the same question more than once, there may be a reason. Assumptions that the customer lacks the education or intellect to understand will kill your brand. Get to the root cause. Make things easier to use, not harder to understand.

5. **Punishing long-term customers.** When policies or procedures are designed to give it all away to new customers and recover those costs from long-term customers, you're not being smart. You're likely hurting the relationship and the customer experience for those who have helped you the most.

Build the Brand

One thing I've witnessed time and again is that the best customer service and the most incredible customer experiences often come from the simplest ideas that are well executed; therefore brands that are built on the premise that everything they do is an investment in the future will outlast brands that feel forced to defend the past.

The best organization cultures and the best brands always build for the future. Most important of all, they never punish the customer.

CUSTOMER SERVICE DANCE MAY WORK

Have you ever asked someone, "Who is the customer?" Your best answer may be, "Everyone." Is the customer-service dance, which means the ability to be flexible, to welcome new ideas, to integrate customer requirements, and much more, appropriate for your business?

It seems ironic or a good example of karma: if you forget about your customers, they'll likely forget about you.

Dancing with your customers is not about fast moves, quick diversions, or peddling snake oil. Just like with real dancing, you won't go far with two left feet. You'll have to get out there and make something happen, even if you feel the rhythm, but your body just moves weirdly.

Customer Service Dance

The best customer service of all may happen when you allow dancing. The customer-service dance may be the ultimate form of feedback, the best of the best in the customer experience. It all happens because you're doing it together.

Businesses that get this right have customer engagement like few others. They're inviting customers to participate. Customers try products, test examples, work with prototypes, debug software, and cocreate everything that happens. In the end, the customer wins.

This model of customer service doesn't promise perfection; it promises an ongoing effort to improve. Information is free flowing, and engagement means loyalty. This valued customer couldn't possibly do better elsewhere because he or she is building it along with you.

When more people join in the experience, it doesn't get worse; it gets even better. No one needs a special invitation, and it catches on. It's a viral experience. It's a club, a membership, or an entire culture.

Forgotten Customers

Most businesses would tell you that they are doing this, but few actually do. It's not so much that they lack effort or desire. It's mostly because they've forgotten who the customer is.

They're either dancing alone or standing on the side, watching others have all the fun.

Best Dancers

Who are the best dancers? Harley Davidson, Dollar Shave Club, and Amazon—your secret is out. Thanks for the dance.

CONSISTENCY MATTERS FOR THE CUSTOMER EXPERIENCE

Have you ever wondered if consistency matters? In your customers' eyes, consistency may be the only thing that keeps them loyal.

Yesterday I had lunch with a coaching client at one of my favorite pizza shops. Knowing that I frequented the shop, the client asked, "Is the pizza good here?" It hit me when I had to pause before answering. There is one significant problem with this pizza shop. It lacks consistency.

Customer Experience

Go to a McDonald's, Burger King, or Pizza Hut anyplace where you can find one. At any of these establishments, you'll have the same or very similar quality of food. You can count on it.

You know how it will taste. The menu may be the same or very similar, and the ambiance will be identical.

Knowing what to expect matters, and consistency may be why we shop, buy, or consume. Inconsistency brings on trust issues and the inability for the customer to recommend the quality.

INCONSISTENCY BRINGS ON TRUST ISSUES AND THE INABILITY
FOR THE CUSTOMER TO RECOMMEND THE QUALITY.

During our lunch, I went on to explain that sometimes the pizza is fantastic, but other times it is just OK. OK isn't always good enough. It may be when the alternatives aren't any better, but when you recognize that there are many lunchtime choices, this pizza shop may lose business.

Consistency Matters

Whatever your business is, trust in the notion that consistency matters.

Consistency may be why people shop, and it is certainly a big part of why they trust. Lack of consistency may signal problems. It detracts from the customer experience.

When organizational leaders or front-line employees don't care enough to make it consistent, customers may not care enough to return. The perceived value drops from exceptional to average, and average is available everywhere.

Authenticity and Loyalty

Loyalty may make a difference, but the ease of purchase somewhere else may outshine loyalty even on a good day.

If you work for a business, an organization, or an institution, is the output consistent? Only when your output is consistent and original is your work good enough to be labeled authentic.

What is not authentic may be considered to be available anywhere. The question then may become, "Are you loyal?"

No one needs to ask why.

THREE REASONS REPACKAGING HURTS

Sometimes it is about a fresh look; other times it is about sustaining or improving profit margins. It may seem like a good idea, but have you considered how repackaging hurts?

I grew up eating breakfast. It was reinforced as the most important meal of the day. Today arguments exist whether breakfast is good or bad, but I'm rolling with the concept that breakfast is a good idea.

Same Face but Different

Most days for as long as I can remember, I indulged in traditional breakfast cereals. Sure, some of them had little marshmallows and were loaded with sugar. Sometimes as a kid, I added sugar. Yes, it is true, and I'm still alive.

Cereal is still in my diet, but what is up with the boxes? I'm not sure if it is applicable to all brands, but many have changed their packaging. The box looks the same from the front, but its thickness has diminished, and so has the product weight.

In retail markets, we often consider the product face. In this case, the product face remains basically unchanged. Its height and width take up just as much space. So the presentation is the same or very similar. The idea may be more profit, but the true cost may be unbearable.

Does the model work? It may in the short term, but when the customer feels cheated, will it still be OK?

Repackaging Hurts

Here are three reasons repackaging hurts:

1. **Hurts trust.** Consumers often make purchases or stick with a brand because they trust it. This is true for nearly everything. It is true with cereal for kids (big kids too), consumer electronics, and automobiles.

2. **Hurts brand.** Not only is this particular product in jeopardy, but so is anything associated with the brand. When trust has been violated, it will often spread to other products or labels produced by the same company.

3. **Loses customers.** With the trust and brand violated, the customer may make a different purchasing decision. This is potentially a lost customer, perhaps lost forever.

Consider cereal to be a metaphorical example. This is true with nearly any product. It may also be true with people.

When you don't get what you expect or you feel fooled, it may be the beginning of something—perhaps the beginning of the end.

Be cautious because repackaging may hurt.

CUSTOMER RANKING: HOW DO YOU RANK YOUR CUSTOMERS?

We often pay attention to one of our best customers, or we sometimes take them for granted. Have you considered the impacts of customer ranking?

Ranking seems like a great idea. It may cause us to pay attention to those transactions that seem more volatile. The customers with the highest ranks may be important, but are they more important than others?

Ranking our customers does seem to have some value. Certainly, telling someone, "You're our number-one customer" may have some value. It may also cause him or her to ask for that special favor. Special favors aren't really the challenge though.

The challenge with ranking our customers may come from the simple mistake of prioritizing how we view our level of service. The most basic value in determining the success of customer service is that the provider shouldn't be the judge and the jury. Truly, the customer is the judge and jury.

Customer Ranking

Does the one-time small-purchase customer turn into your largest account? It may; it is certainly possible.

Have you considered the power of word of mouth? Do the customers who only purchase once in a while have larger connections socially? They may.

On the other hand, do the customers who buy less, say little, and seem to do nothing matter less? It is doubtful, and this may prove to be the slipperiest of all slopes.

Every customer counts; every customer matters. Some do more business, and some do less. If you make the decision to play only with your favorites, you may be missing out.

Your best customers may be the ones who say less to you but tell everyone of their happiness with your business transactions. They may not throw their weight around by asking for special deals or expecting big bonus programs. Most importantly, they may not ask you to bend the rules because they are the best.

Rank Matters

How do you manage customer ranking? Are those with the largest sales, the ones who are the most profitable or have the most transactions, the best? They are all important, but being popular may not mean they are the best.

Remember that the most important rank may be the rank that the customers give to their vendor.

Be very careful how you rank.

THREE REASONS COMMITTEES SHOULDN'T DESIGN CUSTOMER SERVICE

Today much of our customer service has a digital focus. We download, upload, and avoid the printout or hard copy. Digital services really aren't the problem though. It may be more about the design. There are reasons committees shouldn't design customer service.

It is easy for the committee, the board of directors, and those in the ivory tower to get off track. They often design to protect profit while often not realizing that they are limiting the exact scenario they are trying to protect. Certainly, you can't give it all away, but you also need to have the correct focus.

Design Customer Service

Here are three reasons committees shouldn't design customer service:

1. **Operationally feasible.** The committee usually (but not always) represents people across the operational framework. They design what works for operations while seeking solutions to resolve operational problems. Solutions for customers are often not their focus even when they suggest that they are.

2. **Top floor.** We tend to understand our own framework. The front line is often very different from the top floor. Sure, you can see things from the top of the canyon, but that doesn't necessarily mean you'll make the best choice to ride the white water in a raft at the bottom.

3. **Punishment.** There is a delicate balance between helping the customer for more future profit and protecting the bottom line. Elevators and escalators are expensive, but forcing your customers to take the stairs may be more punishment than

they'll accept. Literally or figuratively, committees often decide in favor of the stairs.

Design of the Committee

The argument may then become that the wrong people are on the committee. Certainly, that is a valid argument. That may lead us to consider how the committee formed.

Lack of effort may not be the reason for failure. It may be the design.

IS CUSTOMER SERVICE FOR VENDORS?

A chapter devoted to management or managing and developing a customer-service culture wouldn't be complete without considering the other side of the fence. You have a relationship with vendors; should you approach these relationships with the same kind of courtesy and respect?

Let's be sure we are on the same page. You give a vendor a purchase order, and the vendor gives you an invoice. It isn't the other way around. What about customer-service techniques or etiquette? Does that apply to both sides of a transaction? Is customer service for vendors?

Customer service may mean more than just providing fast, friendly, and kind interactions with your customers. Perhaps it should apply to all scenarios.

Sometimes your vendor may be a website, but chances are good there is still some human interaction somewhere. One of the goals of exceptional customer service is to make people feel good. We strive to make them feel valued, important, and respected.

Vendors are people too. It may matter which side of the transaction you are on, but shouldn't both sides feel good about the business? Of course they should.

Customer Service for Vendors

Here are a few fundamentals that should easily apply from customer to vendor:

- **Courtesy.** Yes, you're likely pushing hard for a great price, exceptional terms, and fast delivery. Negotiation means that both sides are willing to compromise. <u>Negotiating hard</u> makes good business sense, but you can still be courteous in your demeanor.

- **Follow-up.** You expect your vendors to follow up with status. You expect follow-up if they encounter any delays or problems. As the customer, shouldn't you have a responsibility to keep the vendor informed if there are any changes on your end? The answer is easy: yes.

- **Thank-yous.** Who should express thanks and appreciation? You are both in this together. It should be a partnership. Extending kindness, expressing appreciation, and showing that you care is a two-way street.

Do You Choose Sides?

Certainly, the vendor side of any transaction has some differences when compared with the customer side. Do we really need to choose sides? Technically, yes, we do. However, in the spirit of a healthy relationship, it really doesn't matter which side you are on.

Do good business. Be appropriately assertive.

Relationships are about people. Give good service.

CHAPTER 2—SUMMARY

Management choices, perhaps better said as the choices that management makes, will always significantly impact culture. While provocative, I still believe one of the best questions to start a healthy brainstorming session on customer service is "What are you doing that punishes your customers?"

Customers may accept a lot of mediocre performances. When the choices are few and the need is strong, customers will endure quite a bit. Some businesses build their cultures around doing and providing just enough and nothing more. This likely isn't a good philosophy though and one that may be better left to your competition.

Management shapes the culture, whether it is upper management, middle management, or even those leading on the front line. Every decision and every choice have potential consequences. Of course, that includes a choice to do nothing.

Choices are important and so is the voice of the business. Management has a big role with managing the voice. First, the internal voice helps to illustrate the desired culture, and second, with external customers, communication from any employee may represent to the customer all that the organization is and all that it does.

The management of breakdowns in customer service is often quickly identified. The customer may make notification, inventory control might find a discrepancy, or there may be many other signals. Wear down is harder to identify and as such may be even more important. Management should always be on the lookout for both breakdowns and wear downs. More importantly, it should be prepared to take appropriate actions quickly and effectively.

My favorite may be to insist on frequently asking, "What are we doing to punish our customers?" Fix and refine; make things better. Consider the concepts of the customer-service dance to engage and strengthen existing relationships. Surprisingly, the dance may also work to onboard new customers. Today value is more important than ever, and a lack of value, inconsistencies, or the feeling of vendors not caring often has potential customers on the hunt to secure better customer to vendor relationships.

Every customer counts, and every customer matters, and as such customer rank has its merits. Customer rank can be a slippery slope; it needs management to guide the communication, policies, and any processes connected with it. Keep in mind that customers are likely ranking you. Be sure you rank well.

The design of customer-service philosophy should include the right people. It shouldn't be a top-only decision or an operations-only decision. It shouldn't be only a sales, marketing, or front-line team members' decision. It should include everyone; it should be a collaborative design that is customer-centric. If customer-service philosophy is designed in a vacuum, that may be exactly what you get. Metaphorically speaking, you may get a lot of meaningless and sometimes toxic dirt.

Management is largely viewed as an internal scenario—a body that sets policy and procedure and also makes sure that people are held accountable. Certainly, this has relevance and makes much sense; however, what goes on behind closed doors will have much to do with what is reflected to the external customer.

Management may sometimes have the hardest job. Balancing the internal and external, managing communication up the ladder, down the ladder, all while including messages of their own. Management often must navigate sales, operations, accounting, and many other departments defined and categorized by name. Management must always realize that everyone is in it together, and they must act as a role model and encourage this philosophy.

Nobody said it would be easy. Appropriately, pride comes from a difficult job done well.

3

_________INTERNAL

INTERNAL

Ask any unsuspecting employee who their customer is, and most will identify by name or by demographic an external customer. It is common and likely should be expected.

Our reality is that while we sometimes know we should identify internal as well as external, the internal situations are sometimes not so clear. Internal customers represent everyone within the organization. All employees need internal resources. They use them to accomplish the job. They also have a responsibility to provide services to others, and thus we have an internal customer-service relationship.

I would like to suggest that those organizations that truly have a customer-service culture, not just some scattered customer-service behaviors, would be less likely to fall into the trap of only being able to identify the external customers. This is so because if you truly have a culture of customer service and you don't view customer service as only a department or a group, you will likely quickly connect with the idea that everyone is working to support someone else.

Do you have a person who ships products from the warehouse or out the back door? For that individual, the external customer is important, but so is internally serving the sales representative or someone else who he or she is serving since that person is not shipping the product for himself or herself.

Is there a person who manages technology or answers technology questions internally? Then of course the employees at large who run into challenges or difficulties using technology tools may be the customers.

Certainly, it doesn't take long to recognize the internal as well as external customer relationships.

Only the organizations that really strive and dig deep to create a customer-service culture will fully embrace the internal and external relationships. It is a mind-set shift for many of them. They have grown accustomed to the idea that customers are external people, and internal people are merely coworkers or colleagues.

THEY HAVE GROWN ACCUSTOMED TO THE IDEA THAT CUSTOMERS ARE EXTERNAL PEOPLE, AND INTERNAL PEOPLE ARE MERELY COWORKERS OR COLLEAGUES.

Often the businesses or organizations that get this part right—meaning that they have a customer-centric approach that starts on the inside and then is delivered consistently on both the inside and the outside—have a culture of customer service.

What is the culture of your organization? Are you appropriately valuing both internal and external customers? Does everyone understand and recognize this relationship?

IS INTERNAL CUSTOMER SERVICE MORE IMPORTANT?

I believe that we learn the basics of customer service at a very young age. Before we are teenagers, we probably know something about friendliness, kindness, and the power of a smile. We might not realize the linkages of our life experiences to business performance, but the fundamentals of customer service are often present.

All grown up and active in the workforce, we are often reminded of the need for enhancing these fundamental skills, and in our job roles is where it really starts to count. We can recite cliché phrases such as "The customer is always right" or "Customer service is our core value," and we quickly learn that anticipating customers' needs before they ask is when we are performing really, really well.

In seminars, I suggest that there isn't any rocket science associated with customer service, but there is always plenty to learn. It's more than just flashing a smile, being polite, and trying your hardest to meet or exceed expectations. I'm not surprised when participants quickly embrace all the fundamentals, allowing us to dive deeper into skills related to examining needs and creating those lasting, unforgotten impressions. What does sometimes surprise me is that many people in the workforce don't understand the need for internal customer service.

What do you think is more important: internal or external customer service?

Internal customer service in its simplest terms is the practice of creating an exceptional customer-service experience—only instead of focusing on the external customer, we are doing it internally with peers, teams, supervisors, direct reports, and essentially everyone. Someone we've worked around for several months or several years doesn't become someone who we should fail to serve, or disrespect, or in some way devalue or ignore. In fact, he or she may just represent the opposite. It seems easy to get onboard (wrongfully so) with the attitude that someone in another department, work group, or different corporate location really doesn't matter all that much to our personal success; after all, we pride ourselves on putting our (external) customers first.

Communication or miscommunication is often blamed as the root cause for sabotaging the external customer experience, and, of course, there is plenty of evidence lending support to that conclusion. However, one question worthy of finding an answer to is how the actions or behaviors associated with *internal* customer service influence the *external* experience.

Internal customer service is critical for

- creating a "do as we do," not a "do as we say" culture;
- discovering problems first before they go external;
- ensuring that respect and appreciation are core values;
- building foundations for energizing positive experiences; and
- uniting the team and creating a focus on the customer experience.

Perhaps the first step for any organization is to identify what internal customers mean to its success. While there is likely a general workflow and specific positions or workgroups that are designated for internal support, sadly many employees fail to realize what internal customer service really means. Once the entire team understands and is committed to an exceptional internal service experience, the external experience will have the foundational support necessary to drive exceptional results.

In a world of narrow profit margins, competing technologies, and service economy, your most important product may be your ability to create a positive, lasting, never-to-be-forgotten customer experience.

Is internal customer service more important? I think it definitely comes first.

HAVE YOU FORGOTTEN ABOUT INTERNAL CUSTOMER SERVICE?

Ask nearly anyone in business, "Who is your customer?" You're likely to receive an answer that is connected with the external customer. Absolutely the external customer is important, but don't forget about internal customer service.

Taken for Granted

People tend to take a lot for granted. Family, friends, and relations of any kind are often assumed to be both willing and able to withstand disappointments, setbacks, and forgiveness.

Sure, some relationships can withstand nearly anything. Can workplace relationships endure it? Are some organizations missing their marks with internal customer service?

I doubt I'm alone when I suggest that they are. How we treat each other, even those who we've worked around for years, is reflective of the vibe we deliver externally.

Sometimes at first thought, it is difficult for people to connect the dots with coworkers being customers, but it is important. Direct report to boss, peer to peer, or many other combinations exist both up and down the organizational ladder. Does your organization recognize this?

Internal Customer Service

Here are a few simple questions to ask yourself about your delivery of internal customer service:

1. **How do I greet my coworkers?** Greetings set the stage for everything that happens next. It doesn't matter if it is Monday, Friday, or any day in between. If you're dragging yourself around and commenting about how terrible it is to be at work, good luck with having an exceptional customer-service culture.

2. **What are the needs of other employees?** It is not always about reporting relationships. Just because someone is not your boss doesn't mean that you don't go the extra mile to help. Instead of saying, "It's not my job," consider how you can pitch in. Offer to help.

3. **Do I give as much as possible to help support their needs?** It may seem easier to let it be someone else's responsibility, and it is true that it might be. It is also true that sometimes it is

important for everyone to do their own part. However, when you think about their needs, you may find there is more room to give.

4. **Do I leave the door open?** Do you offer your assistance? I hope that you do. Always be sure to close the communication in nearly the same way you have opened it. Offer to always be there to lend a hand. Leave the door open for them to get your willing assistance in the future.

Always Remember

If your culture supports being rude, uncommitted, and lackadaisical in the approach to helping each other internally, what do you think will be reflected externally?

Have you forgotten about internal customer service?

Who is your customer?

TOO BUSY

When you need that catchall phrase to stop the onslaught of additional work, you often say, "I'm too busy."

Too busy can become the main excuse; it seems to work. "Look at everything I have to do, look at the piles on my desk, and look—over there is the work I completed yesterday. If you want me to work on all this other urgent stuff, you can't possibly dump more work on me."

Too busy is also the excuse for not interrupting, no phone calls please, or a signal that the work immediately in front of you is the only work that matters. Too busy is sometimes at its worst in peer-to-peer communication, where it may mean "I'm going to watch you sink as I swim." In nearly all environments, too busy replaces the to-do list, the project database, and the help ticket.

Too busy may be better expressed with some questions.

- What is the priority?
- How soon do you need this?
- Does this lead to more revenue, profit, or our achieving goal?

I've often wondered what happens when you're too busy and all this work goes to the next person on staff, is outsourced, or your customers find another place or person who can serve them better. The only thing worse than your telephone ringing, your e-mail count growing, or getting too many interruptions is to have none at all.

Can you afford to be too busy?

CAN YOU AFFORD THE HIGH COST OF RUDENESS?

Rudeness: we may label it as disrespect, blame it on generational differences, or reference it as extremely poor customer service. Have you thought about the high cost of rudeness in your workplace?

There seems to be a growing trend with rude behaviors. Some may argue that this trend exists mostly because bad behaviors are widely accepted or at least that they are often widely ignored.

Over the years there has been a lot of blame thrown at bad bosses. Certainly, if workplace leaders exhibit rude behavior, it can negatively impact employees. Christine Porath[1] pointed out some of these in her 2015 article "No Time to Be Nice at Work."

Are there additional impacts associated with workplace rudeness?

Learned Behaviors

Rudeness is a learned behavior. We may consider our social interactions, things we witness in public places, and of course the cultural behaviors of our workplace.

We see it on television shows that resemble cartoons, reality TV programming, and many of the modern-day news channels. The same is true for social media, where rudeness may sell with likes and clicks, thumbs-up, or by going viral.

Rudeness seems to sell—and often sell big.

Cost of Rudeness

Does it eventually cost your business or organization? Yes. Some of the costs are buried in employee turnover, loss of customers, and an unfavorable reputation.

There may be other costs too. In one recent example, a major news network encountered at least several harassment suits (*Julie Roginsky v. Fox News former chief Roger Ailes, and current company president Bill Shine*[2]) from employees, former employees, or contributors. True or not true, settled in or out of court, there is a price to be paid.

In any business, the behavior associated with the work environment or customer experience has a price.

For most organizations, it starts with the culture. How an organization communicates, interacts with customers, and treats its employees will have a lot to do with the behaviors that are replicated.

These costs can be minimized with employee-training programs that target improving workplace civility, building a customer-service culture, and developing better leaders.

Affording the Price

There is always a price to be paid. You can use prevention and maintenance that keep your culture in check or hope that things will never break down.

If you believe rudeness costs, prevention and maintenance seem like the logical choice.

If you don't believe it, you may want to consider what happened with United Airlines (Passenger dragged off overbooked United flight[3]) or Allen Kovac (Steven Tyler blasts former manager[4]) before you make your final decision on your budget.

IS KEEPING WORKPLACE COMMITMENTS ENOUGH?

Someone asks the question, "Who can help with this project?" You're interested, passionate about it, and recognize it as an opportunity, so you go for it. Can you keep your workplace commitments?

At least once per week, someone talks with me about being overcommitted (see appendix D, five reasons for overcommitment). Someone else talks with me about the frustration of employees who don't deliver on their promises. What is most surprising is that this is a huge blind spot (see appendix E, blind spots managed) for so many professionals.

People count on other people to deliver. They are expecting a result within a timeline. Schedules and workloads are based around it. Next steps are contingent upon it. Are you delivering?

Expectations

Expectations may be the problem. Remember that although this may be internal, this is likely a customer-service transaction. The key to customer service is meeting or exceeding the expectations of the customer. When the expectations are higher, the performance required is greater.

Internal or external service transactions are never truly measured by you. They are measured by the expectations of the *customer* compared with results as determined *by the customer*.

So the trick really is to understand the customer expectations. Workplace professionals who understand the expectations and are appropriately committed (see appendix F, overcommitted and undervalued) are often able to deliver. That is how they keep their jobs.

Sometimes in an effort to please the boss, gain recognition, or simply out of passion for the project, employees excitedly help to set the expectation too high. In other cases, they simply overcommit.

Workplace Commitments

The next time you raise your hand for the project, volunteer, or suggest that you or your team can do the work or solve the problem, be sure about the timeline. Understand the expectations and the resources required.

Keeping your workplace commitments is expected. *Exceeding expectations is fantastic*; you become the *hero*.

Failure to do either may set you back to a place you don't want to be. It's a single digit. It rhymes with "hero."

HOW YOU TREAT EMPLOYEES DETERMINES YOUR CUSTOMER SERVICE CULTURE

What makes the difference in achieving good customer service when compared with great customer service? Have you ever considered the idea that how you treat employees determines your customer-service culture? Does your organization have any conflicting values?

How You Treat Employees

1. **Greetings.** Are people reporting to work with knuckles dragging, or are they entering with shoulders squared and heads held high? Simple things like smiling and saying hello make a difference. It works everywhere.

2. **Understanding Needs.** Understanding needs is a cultural value that often makes the difference between dictating outcomes or creating a focus of caring and purpose. Being considerate and showing empathy are good values for any customer, internal or external.

3. **Appreciation.** Employees who feel appreciated will often care more about the success of the organization. The same is true for bringing customers back. Customers who feel valued and appreciated will be more loyal and committed. Be thankful, and show lots of appreciation.

4. **Signs and Disclaimers.** Signs, policies, and procedures may be important to serve as guidelines or reminders, but their tone sends the message. The legal stuff is important but often doesn't connect people culturally. Signs or signals of distrust will likely be replicated externally.

5. **Questions Answered.** We all know that communication is critically important. Do your employees have unanswered questions? A lack of information sharing may be the first step toward breakdowns in trust and respect. Certainly, there may be a need for confidentially, but it must be managed respectfully.

6. **Giving Help.** When coworkers need help and no one cares, don't expect any different treatment for your external customers. Giving help and lending a hand is a cultural value. It starts internally and is then delivered externally. Organizations who deliver it externally but not internally have additional challenges.

7. **Energy.** If those in the internal culture complain about Mondays and celebrate Fridays, how is that reflected in the customer experience? Certainly, there are businesses that may have a business advantage to capture these emotions, but for all

other businesses, this may be more of a turn-off rather than a turn-on.

Customer Service Culture

If you're trying to create the best customer experience, you may want to take a look internally. How you treat employees really does matter.

IF YOU'RE TRYING TO CREATE THE BEST CUSTOMER EXPERIENCE, YOU MAY WANT TO TAKE A LOOK INTERNALLY.

The culture that your employees feel and understand may be the same message that they're sending your customers.

CHAPTER 3—SUMMARY

Potentially, a chapter dedicated to internal customer service could also be sarcastically called "Do as I Say, Not as I Do," not because this is the appropriate behavior or cultural value but because it is what is often found behind closed doors.

Any successful venture should have its own house in order before trying to deliver to the external customer. While sometimes the rapid pace of growth and the demands of running a business can get garbled, a conscious effort for balance is helpful.

How we treat each other is important. It is important for courtesy and critical for respect. Organizations who lack trust and respect are often the ones that struggle the most with communication. Communication is often described as being the problem for breakdowns in the customer experience.

Is your house in order? Do you put enough effort into understanding and managing the internal operations and the philosophies connected with the customer experience? Do you care enough?

4
CARING

CARING

Perhaps nothing hits home more than when we feel like somebody, sometimes anybody, cares. Needless to mention, this is an underlying principle of customer service.

After a terrible customer experience, we often find ourselves asking, "Does anyone care?" We may feel so mistreated that we have nothing else to believe except that the business or organization we have just transacted with simply does not care.

It is quite simple really. We have to start at the top. If we are thinking about culture, the organizational leaders have the most responsibility. Sure, everyone must do their parts, but without actions, behaviors, and attitudes that signal caring at the top, the likelihood of developing a culture that cares is nearly nonexistent.

There are countless ways that organizations can show that they care, but most importantly it typically involves putting yourself in the customer's position. What may matter to you? What are you doing that makes it easy for the business but harder for the customer? How are you punishing your customer?

WHAT ARE YOU DOING THAT MAKES IT EASY FOR THE BUSINESS BUT HARDER FOR THE CUSTOMER?

Organizations that truly care place the customer first. Certainly, there must always be consideration for costs and managing the bottom line. What do the customers expect?

In some cases, customers knowingly pay less, and as a result their expectations for exceptional levels of service diminish. If you buy a $15,000 car, you expect it to run and be reliable. If you buy a $50,000 car, you expect a little more. If you're a high roller and spend $100,000 for a car, your expectations are again much different.

Customers expect you to care but typically only at the level consistent with their perceptions of price and value. The danger always is that customer expectations are sometimes hard to measure.

If the $15,000 car buyer expects levels of service and value the same as the $100,000 car, you have a problem. Sometimes educating the customer about volumes, pricing, and differing levels of service is necessary.

Most consumers or your end customer will not be terribly far off from reasonable expectations. After all, they might have shopped around or have a clear understanding that there are differences in price.

It seems that the old rule holds up: you only get what you pay for. I can promise you from my experiences that this is always true.

Do you care? Does the culture of your organization support a caring atmosphere? Are those values and beliefs documented and illustrated to all customers, including both internal and external? Caring is not so much about price, but it is about perceived value, respect, and relationships.

WHAT ARE YOUR CUSTOMER SERVICE ETHICS?

Ethics can be a controversial subject. What seems perfectly fine to one person may be extremely wrong to another. Do you think much about customer-service ethics?

People sometimes believe that it is OK if it is a small thing. It may be the little white lie or the dirt swept under the carpet. In other cases, it may be connected to the concept of a baker's dozen or getting a take-home container after having a full meal at the buffet.

What do you think: Are people and businesses ethically challenged?

Observed Ethical Challenges

Make a cake, and you may hide the imperfections with extra icing—seems sweet enough.

What about the chicken nuggets left over from the lunchtime rush? Did the cook notice or simply not care? Perhaps it is about profit: no nuggets wasted.

The same may be true for the aged lettuce tossed into your salad or cleverly hidden under your sandwich bun. A few pieces here and there—no one will notice.

Ethics exist in customer service. Sometimes they are cleverly disguised in the sale. Other times there is hope that it simply goes unnoticed. Besides, if discovered, there is an apology to make things right.

Is this the food you want to eat? Is it the product you thought you were buying or what you expect to find inside the brown box on your doorstep? No customer wants this surprise.

You Are What You Build

In life, you are the product of your habits repeated over and over again. The same is true for your business reputation. You are the product of what you deliver over and over again.

You may sweeten the cake sometimes and get away with it since icing seems like an extra. Few would probably find fault or feel shortchanged.

Cold nuggets and brown lettuce are never a good idea. Some may complain, but many others will just go somewhere else the next time.

Customer Service Ethics

What you try to hide or pretend to not notice may get you through the day. After all, if no one says anything, did it really happen?

The successful shop, the one that cares and is ethical, is not sweeping anything under the carpet. It is not building it for today. It is building it for today and tomorrow.

Its customers come back and refer others.

WHY DO RETURN CALLS MATTER?

Did you return that telephone call from yesterday? What about the one from two days ago or last week? Do return calls still matter?

My experience in business started before what we know today as the Internet and before most businesses had any kind of voice-mail system. Just for the record, that was the early to mid-1980s, and we did have electricity and automobiles.

I remember when the office supply stores sold a small gadget that sat on your desk; it was about three or four inches tall and resembled a small spear or nail sticking straight up. The purpose of this gadget was to harpoon your "while you were out" message slips. Much like getting "likes" on today's social-media channels, you achieved clout and power by your display of these clever, little, four-by-five-inch, pink "while you were out" messages, and if you were somebody, you got a lot of messages.

During this era, many businesses had a culture that insisted on returning all calls within twenty-four hours. Today, many businesses don't even have a guideline, a recommended practice, or a company policy for returning telephone calls.

Returning telephone calls applied to customers, vendors, intercompany calls, and let's not forget about when the boss called. Yes, you returned the call from someone trying to sell you something; yes, you returned the call when you didn't know who the person was or what he or she wanted; and, yes, you always returned customer calls. You returned nearly all of them, even the interoffice calls and those coming from your boss.

Doesn't this matter to anyone anymore?

Return Calls Matter

Yes, it should, and, yes, it does. While this is somewhat of a personal pet peeve, I hear it from many of my clients too. This is a customer experience story, a reputation statement, and part of your brand.

Granted, a lot has changed, and progress is very important, but never underestimate the power of how you make someone feel.

Many people claim that our world lacks respect and social skills and often fails to honor or uphold commitments. Is any of this a reputation or brand that you want personally or for your business? Can you afford to be without a cultural guideline for returning telephone calls or e-mail messages?

For most, the answers are simple: no and no.

Most people don't like to be spammed; most don't like to get a pushy, unsolicited sales call from someone they don't know; and, yes, most want to be as efficient and productive as possible. I can't name a single business that would openly suggest that it is not concerned about its reputation, its brand, and the customer experience.

Telephone calls or e-mail messages aren't your worst enemy. Not having any is.

RESPONDING SHOWS THAT YOU CARE

Have you thought about how often you hear "He or she never got back to me"? Responding shows that you care. Is it respectful (see appendix G) professional etiquette?

In a fast-paced world of highly competitive markets where costs (prices) are constantly being driven down or minimized, the difference for any organization becomes more about service. Often we label this "customer service." Do people get it?

It's not uncommon for me to talk with my clients about the challenges they face. Typically, somewhere along that path, I'll ask them about customer service. Their mind-sets often connect customer service with the sales team, postsales team, or a low-budget call center.

Here is a news flash. In an economy where price often wins for products that are available everywhere, your entire organization or business is (or should be) built around service. This means that every person who is a touch point for any kind of service, internal or external, needs to be responsive.

Reputation

Your organization is building a reputation and a brand, or else you're tearing one down.

What people say, think, share, type, and click with others will condition future interest to buy products and services or give positive recommendations. People suggest that they get it, but what are their behaviors and habits? Do the people who make up your team or organization respond appropriately?

Here are a few basics:

- What are your communication guidelines? Does every person return *all calls* and *e-mail* (internal or external) within twenty-four hours? If you have respectful guidelines, are they published to the team? What are your cultural behaviors and habits? What does the boss do?

- Use silence strategies sparingly. Business to business with clients and vendors may sometimes feel like dating, but purposely delaying a response because you want to seem busy is not a healthy foundation for business relationships.

- Err on the side of giving a response. Much of our communication today involves e-mail. If someone sends you a quick note and you read it but need more time, say so. If your response is going to be delayed, say so. Sometimes just indicating that you're in receipt of their communication is helpful.

Shows You Care

Chances are good that whether you are being *paid* to just show up or you are being paid to work your tail off, professional etiquette will have a direct impact on your image, and more importantly, the image of the organization that provides your paycheck.

Customer service is not a department; it is a culture.

Responding shows that you care. Be the example. Lead.

The most responsive team wins.

BUILD CUSTOMER RELATIONSHIPS AND LONG-TERM WINS

Sometimes the problem with "get the deal now" is that it doesn't build anything. When you're trying to build customer relationships, are you focused on a short-term fix or long-term gain?

Get the dime in your pocket now and worry about tomorrow later might sometimes seem like the best tactic. After all, you've achieved a win. Leading early is often good, but it doesn't guarantee you'll finish the race or win the game.

Short-Term Fix

Sometimes the short-term strategy creates a long-term loss.

You may push to close a sale even when it doesn't align with the customer need. Perhaps you'll get your way with a suggestion of scarcity.

SOMETIMES THE SHORT-TERM STRATEGY CREATES A LONG-TERM LOSS.

Alternatively, you may try to shove your way around with fear by pushing hard for the extended warranty. As a final stand, you may jump up and down, pitch a fit, or hold your breath until you get a yes.

When your short-term strategy is over, will you still have any long-term customers?

Build Customer Relationships

There are a lot of businesses that don't have continuous daily transactions with the same customer.

When the real-estate agent, the plumber, and the consultant are doing their jobs right, it isn't about a one and many; it is more about a one and done. With a job well done, their customers may not come back around for many months or even years.

When you're considering the customers' experience, their satisfaction, and relationship longevity, it has to be built on long-term values, not on short-term wins.

Your culture and brand aren't built overnight, and neither is your reputation.

When you're building a lasting impression, creating long-term value, and doing it with customers who trust you, you'll create the kind of win you need. You'll create a customer experience where the story of your quality and commitment is told over and over again over time.

The thing of it all is people still talk, and more importantly, they get social online. Some proclaim that word of mouth is now *world* of mouth. I think they're right. What talk will you create?

Long-Term Win

A quick fix or short-term win to put a dime in your pocket today may not be a long-term win. In fact, it could have the biggest cost of all.

Build customer relationships, and go for the long-term win.

USING APPRECIATIVE INQUIRY TO BUILD A BETTER CUSTOMER EXPERIENCE

Every business and successful organization cares about the customer experience. Can you use appreciative inquiry methodologies to build a better customer experience?

Those reading who are new to appreciative inquiry only need to understand a few basics about the definition to get started.

Appreciative Inquiry

Appreciative inquiry may be described as a method to search for, uncover, and bring out the best in people, teams, and entire organizations.

Perhaps the most important factor for getting started is to understand that appreciative inquiry is not centered on identifying problems. It is centered on asking questions (inquiring) about what gives a system and its people life.

Consider that it's looking for positive imagination (dreaming) and innovative ways (designing) to use positive approaches. It is not focused on negativity, what didn't or won't work, and chronic diagnoses of what is causing problems.

Based on either a 4-D[1] or 5-D[2] Appreciative Inquiry cycle model, properly empowered people can ask questions, innovate, form strategies, and transform systems and culture based on positive, life-giving forces.

Customer Experience

It's easy to get started on ways to improve the customer experience. Instead of asking customers or the people in your organization what is wrong or what didn't work, use an appreciative inquiry approach.

Consider asking a somewhat vague opening question that will drive the conversation, something like "What would our best product or service, considering no limitations or barriers, look like?"

You can then supplement the interactions with supporting information-gathering questions like:

- What customer stories, testimonials, or other narratives can be shared about best experiences?

- Describe the features or values about our products or services that inspire recommendations to others.

- What brings our customers back for repeat business?

Appreciative Strategies

Often one of the most important and challenging aspects of driving change within a system or organization through appreciative inquiry is carefully and closely monitoring the interactions. Many people, especially those unfamiliar with the process, will quickly digress into problems, reasons why not, and subjective negativity.

During most interventions, this is not intentional to undermine the process. It is more representative of patterns of learned behaviors, which are to identify the problem, exploit it, analyze it, agonize over it, and repeat. That is not the appreciative inquiry way.

Can you use appreciative inquiry approaches to build a better customer experience? Yes.

CUSTOMER SERVICE SURPRISES COME FROM EXPECTATIONS

Many workforce professionals will tell you that they know and understand customer service and satisfaction. After all, they've been witnessing and interacting with service experiences since they were children. What customer-service surprises do your customers experience?

Surprises develop from a difference between expectations and outcomes. Expectations are likely set by your promise. The best question may be, Should you manage from a standpoint of lower expectations or higher expectations?

Lower Expectations

Lower expectations represent the model of you get what you get and you value doing business with us because of it. This may be the fast-food burgers-and-fries restaurants, or it may be the web-based commodity product sales with no telephone number.

Most people doing business there recognize the limitations, and they are OK with that. Their expectations are lower, and their satisfaction may be high.

In these scenarios, the promise clearly expresses the limitations and sets the expectations for quality, price, and, yes, customer service. It may be the "all sales are final" model, but you'll take the chance and feel satisfied. Success in this model is always dependent on high volume.

Higher Expectations

In a higher-expectations model, you are always striving to create the wow moments for the customer. You may feel forced by the competition to raise the bar because you want to maintain profits and be the go-to resource.

YOU MAY FEEL FORCED BY THE COMPETITION TO RAISE THE BAR BECAUSE YOU WANT TO MAINTAIN PROFITS AND BE THE GO-TO RESOURCE.

In this model, managing higher expectations and keeping your promise are part of the vision. The idea is that customers are willing to pay for better quality and higher levels of service. They'll be loyal because you are worth it.

The challenge here may be maintaining the proper focus, finding the right balance, and staying within budget. You may also have to consider how you'll manage your workforce talent to ensure that the ongoing promise is kept.

Customer Service Surprises

One of the most important things in either model is to carefully consider your offer. What is your promise, and does your customer base (or the one you want to create) have lower or higher expectations? What examples will you illustrate, and what expectations will you create?

Managing your message is always important. Remember that their expectations are likely driven by what they *perceive*, which may not be exactly the same as *what you say or mean*.

In either model, the customer-service surprises should always come from exceeding expectations. This is the only surprise they'll accept.

Whatever promise you've made, you'll have to keep. Your customers expect it.

CHAPTER 4—SUMMARY

Revenues and profit margins are absolutely critical. Having a culture that cares is just as important. Sometimes the philosophy is presented as "we are in business to make a lot of money." A strange thing happens with businesses who embrace this philosophy. Many of them also recognize that in order to make a lot of money, they have to care about the customer.

The ball sometimes gets dropped in private businesses that are on their second or third generation of family ownership and in others too. The culture begins to shift. Original values or core beliefs start to grow stale. Sales and revenues continue largely from longevity and long-term customers.

Lose the culture of caring and you'll eventually lose the business. Caring isn't what you say it is; it is what the customers feel. Internally and externally, it is their perception that matters. You may believe you have the best service on the planet. If the customers don't feel it, it simply doesn't exist.

Make caring a part of your culture, and understand your customers. This is your best bet for getting delivery to align with their perception. It is never the other way around.

5
CULTURE

CULTURE

Today for SEO (search engine optimization), it is often said that content is king. Others may change the phrase by saying that content is everything. In your workplace, regardless of the type of business or organization, I may suggest that culture is everything.

People talk about culture often. It is thrown around at the staff meeting and at the retreat, but what is your culture? If you haven't asked yourself that question lately, then you may be overdue.

The single biggest way to improve customer service for your business is to have a culture of customer service. When you are so committed to customer service that your actions and behaviors represent a customer-service mind-set, you're going to have strong representation externally too. It will flow and just seem to be natural.

One problem that often disrupts this mind-set is the delicate balance between delivering exceptional levels of customer service and maintaining or improving the bottom line.

Customer service costs in the short run. It costs employees time, which we know is money, but it often costs in other add-ons, advertising, marketing, and other areas. Long-run value needs to be the focus for having an exceptional customer-service culture.

LONG-RUN VALUE NEEDS TO BE THE FOCUS FOR HAVING AN EXCEPTIONAL CUSTOMER-SERVICE CULTURE.

It may be the cherry on your ice-cream sundae, the chocolate on your pillow in the hotel room, or the upgrade to expedited shipping for your online purchase. Short-term costs are higher, and profit is less, but in the long term, those little fringe benefits are expected to add up. Do they?

Measuring customer-service success can sometimes cross over into advertising and marketing efforts, but otherwise the metrics for measurement should be clear.

Customer service should be clear and intentional. The low-cost online shopping experience may have a model that includes slow shipping. Customers pay less, and they expect less. Other models that are moderate- or high-price experiences have different customer expectations. So understanding who you are as a business and your model is critically important. Not all philosophies or cultures are the same and not all customers are attracted to a specific model.

One of the fundamentals for delivering exceptional service is to recognize that the customer experience is based on perception and expectations. You and your organization should strive to be the very best representation of price and value.

Do you have a culture of customer service?

CUSTOMER SERVICE CULTURE, NOT A DEPARTMENT

Chances are good that your mission statement has something reflecting the importance of the customer. Does your business have a customer-service culture or a department?

Well-intending businesses everywhere believe that they are customer focused, but are they? Let's face it; we probably hear about a few customer-service problems each week. Family, friends, social-media users, and other people talk about breakdowns in the customer experience. When your job is directly connected transaction by transaction to maintaining the customer experience, you probably hear more than just a few. Is your organization customer focused? Does it have a customer-centric approach?

Not a Department

"I have a problem." You need to connect with customer service.

"I want to exchange this shirt I received as a gift." You'll need to take it to the back corner of the store. Follow the signs for customer service.

"I opened the box, and what I ordered is broken." Let me transfer you to customer service.

Big Not Better

Many businesses grow just big enough to forget about the customer. It's true; when the business is young and small, it is cared for, but when it starts to mature, it is sometimes left to fend for itself.

People rightfully believe that leadership starts at the top. Leadership, like customer service, is not a department. Both are about culture.

Success of the business is important and often requires layers of leadership as it grows. However, if the leadership team begins to spend more time behind the double doors of the C suite and less time on continuously building a customer-service culture, something *will* get lost.

Customer Service Culture

Organizational culture is mostly about the values and beliefs of people, the team, and a group. Its concepts are collective and hopefully inspirational.

The people and systems that give an organization life are based on what individuals feel and see. Your customers have expectations that are also based on what they feel and see. It's not what you say; it's what they experience.

YOUR CUSTOMERS HAVE EXPECTATIONS THAT ARE ALSO BASED ON WHAT THEY FEEL AND SEE.

One problem with the business that grows bigger but not better is that it loses its focus on the customer. Leaders stop talking to the front line. They stop spending their time working directly with the people who develop or deliver. Worst of all, they lose track of the customer.

Their feedback systems are all wrong. Their scope of focus is based on digits and dividends. Often they are trying to please the wrong people.

Build It to Last

Make customer service about a lasting culture. Stay connected to where things started.

Don't put customer service in a box. It isn't a department. It's a culture.

HOW TO BUILD BETTER CUSTOMER SERVICE STARTING NOW?

When you ask about customer service, most will tell you that it should be easy. It's true; in concept, customer service is not that hard. In practice, customer service is a little more difficult. Do you know how to build better customer service?

Measuring Customer Service

People often walk blindly with the belief that they have great service. The belief is that they create it with "please" and "thank you" or by kindness and caring. Management often believes that it is created by careful monitoring, pushing out surveys, and collecting feedback.

In some scenarios, exceptional service is measured by sales results and revenue growth, numbers that are typically anchored in historical data or management expectations.

All of those may provide some value, but none of them really tackles the hard stuff. The hard stuff is having a culture of caring and being driven for excellence—not because you say it is so but because your customers know that it is so.

A culture of the best service is built around people who are energized by working together to create an exceptional experience every time. The values and beliefs of those functioning within it create outputs day in and day out that are the standards they live by.

Perhaps the most coveted culture inspires peers to help peers and is one where everyone takes the lead and following or coproducing is natural. The purpose is not to create more followers. It is to create more leaders.

These are their habits, replicated over time.

Build Better Customer Service

Customer service is not validated by the automated return call, the lengthy register receipt with a URL, or simply by asking those who are willing to answer. It's validated when people come back or when they tell others about their positive experiences. Better yet, it is validated when they bring friends the next time.

Customer service is not defined by rules, policies, and ultimatums. That is the easy stuff. It is what nearly everyone does, and it is why there are so many complaints.

Size doesn't matter, but feelings and perceptions do. Shortcuts, fake smiles, and direction pointers aren't providing service. At best they are earning a paycheck.

When you measure against the average or the organization that is just one step ahead, the best you'll ever become is number two.

If you want to build better customer service, you may want to think less about rules and policies and more about culture and caring.

WHEN COMMUNICATION DRIVES CUSTOMER SERVICE CULTURE

Ask an organization about its customer service, and it'll often tell you a lot. It's not uncommon that it believes that it is doing great or at least doing OK. Does internal communication drive customer-service culture?

Occasionally when I'm working with clients, I may ask how they measure customer service. It is not uncommon to get responses such as the following:

"No worries; if we screw something up, our customers let us know."

"We send out a survey every month; responses are typically very favorable."

"We get a lot of feedback; most of it is positive."

Some customers never complain, some will never fill out a satisfaction survey, and some will elect not to tell you of a shortcoming. However, they may tell a dozen of their friends.

Internal Communication

Customer service is driven, at least in part, by internal communication. Communication and the culture of the organization set the tone for the customer experience.

Here are three common communication and cultural pitfalls:

- **Sales performance.** The logic here is that sales performance is OK. If it were really bad or slowing, we might have to dig deeper to understand if we have a customer-service problem. Since most of the feedback offered by customers is good and our sales are stable or growing, we're doing OK. Just keep doing what we're doing.

- **Customer education.** Sometimes the belief is that the customers are not very smart. They wouldn't be having problems if they only knew how to use the product or its associated tools. Certainly, sometimes educating the customer is important, but assuming that the customer will figure it out is a dangerous proposition. Inappropriately stereotyping ignorance may be the fastest way to lose market share.

- **Accepted quality.** Striving for exceptional quality requires constant effort. It may also require reworking and do overs. Forcing your customers to make your (inferior) quality their quality is never a good idea. Customers may accept a lot of levels of quality, but when your quality doesn't measure up, they may go somewhere else.

Customer Service Culture

What do you hear in your organization? What is the internal communication?

"Sales are OK. We're doing OK."

"The customer is an idiot."

"Looks good enough; ship it, and we'll see what happens."

What is the talk? Communication drives culture.

CUSTOMER SERVICE BEST PRACTICES: THREE CULTURAL TIPS

Name just about any business or organization, and you'll be naming an entity that needs exceptional customer service. Have you thought about your customer-service best practices?

So much of our economy today is based on businesses that sell commodity products or services—things that people can get easily and get just about anywhere. In a commodity marketplace, things like price, convenience, and customer service will have a lot to do with revenues.

I often suggest to clients that their product may not be exactly what they think it is. Their true product may actually be their level of customer service.

I OFTEN SUGGEST TO CLIENTS THAT THEIR PRODUCT MAY NOT BE EXACTLY WHAT THEY THINK IT IS. THEIR TRUE PRODUCT MAY ACTUALLY BE THEIR LEVEL OF CUSTOMER SERVICE.

Tips Connected with Culture

Best practices may vary a little depending on the type of business or organization, but here are three of my favorites:

1. **Set standards.** When you consider that customer service is a culture, not a department, it is important for all employees to understand a set of standards. Consider the usual things like return policies, follow-up times, and the ease of interaction with your organization. You'll also need to define what makes you special.

2. **Inside out.** Your customer-service culture starts on the inside. The culture of your organization will have a lot to do with the culture of your customer service. Value employees, constantly reinforce their worth, and connect them to the customer experience. Employees who connect with and understand their purpose will transfer those vibes to the external customer.

3. **Listen, listen, and listen.** One of the best and most important competencies for delivering exceptional customer service is being a good communicator. Many times people want to be the talker, especially those who are very assertive and who lead with a sales mind-set. Instead, ask more questions. Start to understand your customer. The customer wants to be heard. Listen.

Customer Service Best Practices

What are your customer-service best practices?

When you focus on creating a culture of customer service, your customers will notice.

So many businesses fail to follow up and engage with their customers after the sale. Others may appear hurried and lack patience.

Be different. Build trust. Bring value.

Deliver your best practices. Make it your culture.

WHY CUSTOMER SERVICE IS WINNING?

Some organizations view customer service as an expense to minimize.

Customer service is not about a department; it is about a culture. Delivering exceptional customer service is winning.

Winning to Lose

Businesses may sometimes be brutal with sales efforts. The pressure from management or the business owner creates pushy behaviors from account executives or others whose job performance and paychecks depend on closing the sale.

An intense focus on the close of the sale without a similar focus on the customer likely has a cost associated with it. When the push is too hard, it becomes a shove. People seldom forget a shove.

You may win the sale today, but this win may become a loss since it is at the expense of no sale tomorrow.

In a big city or small town, you'll rarely only interact once. The reputation you're building is important. Future decisions to buy goods or services will be at stake. Your individual presence and the culture of customer service that you've demonstrated will always matter.

Customer Service Is Winning

Here are a few things to remember about why customer service is winning:

- **Reputation.** You're not just managing today's transactions; you're building tomorrow's reputation. This reputation will be a factor that is discussed any time someone mentions a need for what you provide.

- **Trust.** People engage with trusted resources. Consider that trust is earned, not just given. Price always matters, but trust is part of your value. Even in transactional sales, trust will play a role.

- **Connection.** Beyond trust is the connection. It will only be a one and done if the perceived value is low. The service you provide may represent part of the sales team you never realized that you had.

Culture Matters

Most organizations will tell you about their exceptional levels of customer service. It's not what they tell you that really matters. It's what they show you.

CUSTOMER SERVICE RULES AND MISUNDERSTOOD COSTS

It happens all the time: something affects profits or progress, and the organization makes a new rule. Does it make sense to make customer-service rules from one bad example?

Nearly every business will tell you that it values the customer. They all cite examples of how hard they work at delivering an exceptional customer experience. Do they live up to doing what they say?

DO THEY LIVE UP TO DOING WHAT THEY SAY?

Certainly, every organization needs to protect itself against fraud, deceit, or profit erosion. They all need customer-service rules but at what cost?

Customer Service Rules

In the early 1980s, I worked in a retail drugstore. I stocked shelves, unloaded trucks, swept the floors, and sometimes worked at the checkout register. At the time, this retail drugstore chain was doing very well, with many stores and lots of valued customers.

Somewhere along the way, some smart folks in district or regional management came up with a new rule. The new rule was that every purchase had to go in a bag, and the receipt had to be stapled to that bag—no excuses, no exceptions.

What a disaster.

Rules in Action

One day as I nervously worked the checkout register while the regional manager looked over my shoulder, I allowed a repeat customer to take his pack of cigarettes and a candy bar (after paying) and leave the store with receipt in hand—no bag, and certainly no receipt stapled to it. Immediately I was summoned to the back of the pharmacy. I was scolded and sent back to the register.

What management didn't realize was that for whatever reason it invented this rule, it was hurting the customers.

We had repeat customers come in every day to make purchases from a candy bar, to cigarettes (big in those days), to a magazine or newspaper. They never returned anything or made a large purchase. They loved the store, and they didn't really need a bag.

These loyal customers loved it right up until the moment management started hurting their experience.

More Than a Job

I was probably only seventeen or eighteen years old, but I knew better. I saw what was happening; it was ridiculous.

Regional management never seemed to get it. The local managers did, but they were under strict guidelines from regional and corporate management.

It was supposed to be a job, but really it was the start of my education. I miss those days—you know, happy customers and all.

THE LOW COST OF CUSTOMER SERVICE

Sometimes the price of progress sounds expensive, and doing nothing feels like the most attractive option. However, doing nothing may have the highest cost of all. Have you considered the low cost of customer service?

You may feel too tired to brush your teeth. You may be in too much of a hurry to change the oil in your car. Moreover, who really needs the security software upgrade?

The truth is that the best time for any of those things is before you encounter a problem.

After the dental cavity, after the check engine light, and after your PC is locked up, it is much harder. It will be much more difficult to turn the situation around and certainly much more expensive.

Maintain or Replace

Most people will quickly identify with the concept that establishing new customers is much more expensive than maintaining them. Most businesses will tell you that they recognize this and that it is an underlying principle they live by. If this is true, what is the budget?

Is there a budget for your dental care, a budget for your oil change, and a budget for software upgrades? Frankly, it will cost less to maintain than to replace, yet sometimes these items slip through the cracks.

Cost of Customer Service

What should be in your customer-service budget? Probably many things, but here are three that are often taken for granted:

- **Training.** Sometimes the more we know, the less we do. Conceptually we often have a good idea of how to care for the customer, but do we really do it? Training sometimes is about building, maintaining, and reinforcing habits. It's not always about discovery.

- **Appreciation.** Appreciation is not a day, a sale, or a clever slogan. Appreciation is a feeling. Invest some of your budget into showing your customers how much you care. It may be as simple as a thank-you, or it may be something they value and didn't expect.

- **Adding Value.** Yes, value is connected to price, but it may not always be hidden in the bar code. Value often has a direct connection to quality and the cost of ownership. In any customer relationship, it starts with the customer experience.

Low Cost

What is your budget for maintaining customers? Your cost of customer service may be lower than you think. It will cost you less to maintain than it does to repair or replace.

Some may say, "I already know this." If you know it, are you doing something about it?

CHAPTER 5—SUMMARY

Culture is a set of values and beliefs. It is about symbols and traditions. It has to do with language, customs, and observed behaviors. Do you understand your culture?

The greatest opportunities still exist right in front of us. In a world where politeness and common courtesy often feel missing or underdelivered, there exists opportunity.

Business models are often similar—the products more representative of a commodity. Goods and services are readily available online, and price will always play a role. The most important feature an organization can have may be its delivery of customer service.

When the customer experience is what drives processes and procedures and sets the values and standards of delivery by systems and people, the organization will thrive. Those that choose to play by another set of rules will be forced to compete only on price, an undesirable situation for most.

Price sometimes wins in the short term. When there is no investment in the customer, there will probably be little investment in the employee, and when there is no investment in either of these, the lowest price will win—until it doesn't. Then everything changes.

Customer service has never been more important and the expectations never more profound. Improve your customer service. Do it for your career, for your department, or for the entire organization.

It is about choice. Choose wisely.

APPENDICES

APPENDIX A

WORKFORCE GENERATIONS DESCRIPTIONS

Traditionals	Born	1930–1945
Baby Boomers	Born	1946–1964
Gen Xers	Born	1965–1976
Millennials	Born	1977–1994
Gen Zers (Gen 9/11, iGen)	Born	1995–

Much debate still exists among generational experts on the date ranges for the most recent generations. Many experts are of the belief that Gen Z may actually start closer to 1990 or 1991.

You can find additional information about the workforce generations in my 2015 book, *Forgotten Respect: Navigating a Multigenerational Workforce.*

APPENDIX B

COMMUNICATING WITH THE C SUITE

It can be elusive, scary, and a place where people sometimes go and are never seen again. Some people will work for most of their careers striving to get to the C suite; others prefer to avoid it.

Is it harder to communicate with those occupying the tower of the elite? If you're not in the tower, the feeling just might be an overwhelming yes.

What makes it so difficult? Aren't these just people?

Yes, of course, but their charge is somewhat different. Sure, everyone is working toward some contribution for the greater good of the organization, but those in the C suite are operating under a different kind of pressure. Their pressure is intense, their time very limited, and often they face decisions for setting directions that could result in an enormous victory or become the harshest defeat.

Do you have success communicating with the C suite? Are you looking for ways to improve it?

Here are a few tips that may help:

1. **Be straightforward.** Time is critical for everyone, and those in the C suite are definitely concerned about time. Details, drama, or indecisiveness tends to slow things down, and time often feels like it is already working against them. Dance less, and give it to them straight.

2. **Bring evidence.** Opinions are not facts. If you're seeking permission or direction for a decision, it may help to have a little proof in your proposal. Statistics, white papers, or stock reports may help your cause, but so will street-smart news reports or details about a marketing campaign recently launched by a competitor.

3. **Be compelling.** If you deliver like a church mouse, you're probably not commanding enough respect. Chances are good that arrogance is too much, but having appropriate confidence, showing passion for your thoughts or ideas, and having a concise delivery will help bring clarity to your message.

4. **Deliver trusted information.** There is a good chance that your C suite executive needs more information, but his or her challenge is getting the right information. The data need to be reliable and valid. Often these executives are provided with so much information from so many different resources that they simply don't know who or what to trust. Become that trusted resource.

5. **Be patient.** While the C suite often operates at a lightning pace, it may seem like a turtle race to others in the organization. If you're going to build a strong relationship with those in the tower, you're going to have to learn to be patient. What feels urgent to you may have a very low priority for them. When in doubt, stay calm and be patient.

Communication drives all that we do. The very best organizations have great communicators from the top to the bottom and from the bottom to the top.

Avoidance, hesitation, or procrastination likely won't improve the outcomes of any communication, especially communication with the C suite.

Make sense? Sweet—you've got this!

APPENDIX C

GENERATIONAL DEFINITION TRAP

If you have fallen into this trap, it's OK; many people have. The generations are not about age; they are about birth year.

Even the first newborn baby brought into the world in this year is getting older, but that doesn't mean that when this baby turns fifty, fifty-five, or sixty years old, he or she will become a baby boomer.

Today traditionals in our workforce are those around seventy-two years old or older. Both Hillary Clinton and President Donald Trump are very near the baby boomer boundary (Hillary was born 1947, President Trump in 1946), but in a year or two, they won't be traditionals. They will always be baby boomers.

People discussing generational differences sometimes fall into the trap of relating generations to age when in reality what is really important is birth year. The shaping of the generations is created through many factors; the three most common are as follows:

1. Major shifts in socioeconomic conditions
2. Major shifts in technology
3. Times of significant turmoil, such as war

Also critical for generational differences are things like rural versus urban living, geographic location, and espoused family values. It is important to understand that for exactly the reasons just described, countries other than the United States will likely experience their own differences when defining their generations.

While all of this sounds very simple, it is one of the most common mistakes I hear when discussing generational differences with people. Just because we are all getting older doesn't mean our generational definition will change.

Let's get it right before we get too old.

APPENDIX D

FIVE REASONS FOR OVERCOMMITMENT

Most people in the workforce want to give their jobs and careers the best they have to give. They work hard and smart and are committed. Can trying to do too much be hurting your career?

During my career, I've run into a lot of interesting things in the workplace—at first glance situations that are almost unbelievable. People sometimes say that love is blind. People who are trying really hard to be impressive in their jobs may sometimes have blind spots too.

Just like too many donuts, hot wings, or trips to the Chinese buffet, overcommitment may be hurting, not helping, your situation.

Hurting Your Career

Here are five reasons:

1. **Can't do everything.** Many people are trying to impress. They raise their hands to take on projects with no real consideration that they may be taking on too much. This also sometimes happens when people are bored with their duties. They volunteer for other assignments, making them too busy for their regular duties.

2. **Connects you with weaknesses.** Just because you like to do it doesn't always guarantee that you are good at doing it. Many people like to sing in the shower or at the karaoke bar. That doesn't mean they should quit their day jobs. In the workplace, people connect you with your work. If your work isn't the best, what people may see is incompetence.

3. **Working twice as hard.** You may have to work twice as hard or twice as long as someone with the natural talent or skills to do the same work. Certainly, if it is an interest for you and you're willing to work hard at it, you may be able to achieve success. Just make sure you're making the most of your natural (or developed) talents and abilities.

4. **Defensive positions.** I can't even begin to express how harmful it may be to take on work or assignments just because you want to block someone else from doing it. This is competition gone too far. Sometimes people will volunteer for roles or tasks simply because they don't want someone else to have an opportunity to shine. Terrible.

5. **Poor response times.** Communication challenges may be the root cause of nearly every workplace problem or issue. They are also responsible for a lot of missed opportunities, mistakes, and poor customer service. When you're overcommitted, you're likely coming up short on call backs, e-mail, and follow through. It's probably also hurting your professional relationships.

Do Great Things

Caring about your career is excellent. Striving to do a great job is excellent. Offering to help or get involved for the greater good of the organization is excellent. Being overcommitted for any reason may be one of the biggest blind spots impacting your career success. It doesn't make you look good; it makes you look bad.

Your biggest struggle may be finding the right balance without crossing any lines. Have you ever felt overcommitted? Could it be a blind spot that is hurting your career?

APPENDIX E

BLIND SPOTS CAN BE MANAGED, RIGHT?

How do you recognize blind spots? It seems realistic that you don't know what you don't know, but what should you do?

Everyone probably has some blind spots, something with their personalities, their drive, or their leadership abilities that they just don't see or else they fail to acknowledge.

First Steps

If you're looking for personal improvement, you may consider that you have at least two areas to assess. You'll have to manage what you know that you don't know, and you'll have to learn more about what you don't know that you don't know.

Sounds a little tricky, but consider thinking about it like this. You may recognize that you need to learn more about being an effective communicator or managing conflict. You'll also probably recognize that you'll have to set some specific goals to improve your skills and reduce wasted time, effort, or other inefficiencies. This is what you recognize that you don't know or that needs improvement.

Blind spots are different because they represent something you don't know or recognize. Otherwise, they fall into the first category and they aren't really blind spots, right? Blind spots may require you to become more socially aware, ask others for feedback, or consider some careful self-reflection.

Recognizing Blind Spots

In the workplace, we may have some common areas for blind spots. Here are a few of them:

- **Ineffective Decisions.** You jump in too quickly, or you fail to consider data, input, and benchmarks. Of course the opposite can be true too. You overanalyze or inappropriately anchor to input, observations, or past experiences.

- **Goal Management.** You set unrealistic goals or goals that may be attainable only with increased resources, capital investments, or time; none of which you have. This results in chronic failures, setbacks, and reduced morale.

- **Perfectionism.** A belief that you have to be perfect at everything, causing burnout for yourself and your team or creating a feeling that nothing is ever good enough. Time may be wasted or misused.

- **Poor Listening.** This is failure to solicit input from others or a belief that others have little to offer, as well as failure to discern fact from opinion. Poor listening is listening to respond instead of listening to understand.

- **Wrong Focus.** This is a chronic focus on issues or problems that aren't directly connected to the goals or mission, perhaps being concerned only with a personal agenda instead of what is best for the group.

Managing Blind Spots

No joke, the first step may be admitting or recognizing that a blind spot exists; this is often half the battle. Once you know of a blind spot, you'll need to take the appropriate corrective action.

Consider how you may learn more. Find articles, books, podcasts, or videos that relate to appropriate corrective actions. Attend workshops and seminars, or select related sessions at an annual conference or convention. Too often people attend sessions that they like but that may not be what they need.

Get coaching and mentoring, or otherwise seek feedback and recognize that although sometimes painful to hear, others may have a point or they may be right. Stay open minded and reflective; not all feedback is well constructed or appropriate, but be receptive to listening more.

Be committed that there is more to know and there are ways to grow. Focus on developing your greatest talents while also improving some weaknesses.

Can blind spots be managed? Yes, when they are recognized.

APPENDIX F

OVERCOMMITTED, UNDERVALUED

What many people really want is a commitment. What they expect is what you promised. When you try to express your value by showing your overwhelming commitment, the best thing that can happen is that you prove your worth, but sometimes what happens is that you prove you were overcommitted. The result of overcommitment is that you may be undervalued.

The overcommitted administrative assistant, supervisor, or emerging executive doesn't show value; he or she shows incompetence. Ouch! At least that may be the perception held by others since their expectations were not met.

Overcommitted

An overflowing bucket lacks value; the perception is that a bigger bucket is necessary. A bucket half full lacks value; it is not being used or has too much waste. An empty bucket is likely the worst of all. A bucket filled just right, the one carrying the most without any waste, not too big, not too small, and delivering exactly as promised, is the most valued bucket of all.

Undervalued

Commit to doing too much while accomplishing less and you are undervalued. Commit just right.

APPENDIX G

EARNING RESPECT: DO YOU PUSH OR PULL?

Ask people how respect is achieved, and many will suggest that it is earned. One thing to remember about respect is that much like success, the definition of it varies. What about you? Are you earning respect?

As a business consultant, I stumble upon some very interesting things from time to time. About eight years ago, I was on assignment working with a midsized manufacturing firm, helping approximately thirty midlevel managers improve their leadership skills. The training project consisted of five different sessions spread across several months.

Before the work began, I was cautioned about a baby-boomer manager who was a great employee but was known to be too tough. The turnover ratio in his area of oversight was much higher than that of other managers. My warning was that he might get "tough" during the course of the seminars.

I like a challenge and was ready to embrace it. He was easy to pick out. He sat near the front of the group but close to the aisle with his arms folded across his chest and a scowl on his face. He appeared engaged but didn't really participate or ask questions, at least not at first.

Earning Respect

During our second session, I was presenting some material on workplace motivation and respect. At one point, I said, "In today's workplace, you can't just ask people to drop and give you twenty." This of course meant to do twenty push-ups.

Then he spoke. "Exactly how are we supposed to motivate these people then? Tell us; how do we do it?" I was surprised but delighted that he spoke up.

My first reaction was to say, "You need to approach them differently. You need to think about motivation differently."

His response, gruff and perhaps slightly sarcastic, was "Well, that sounds good, but how do we do that?"

I thought for a moment and then said, "What if they get all their work accomplished according to their goals, and then you drop and give them twenty?" Many of his colleagues broke out in laughter and added comments like, "Yeah, how about that? You give them twenty."

Push or Pull

Here is the greatest part of the story. Not only did we discover new respect for each other, but he also understood that respect often is not able to be pushed. Respect is defined differently by each individual, and it is largely earned, not given. If you want to create mutual respect, it is best to do it through pull.

Are you earning respect?

NOTES

NOTES

CHAPTER 1

1. *Wikipedia*, s.v. "Blockbuster," accessed August 22, 2017, https://en.wikipedia.org/wiki/Blockbuster_LLC.

2. *Wikipedia*, s.v. "Jeffrey Hayzlett," accessed August 22, 2017, https://en.wikipedia.org/wiki/Jeffrey_W._Hayzlett.

CHAPTER 3

1. "Christine Porath," ChristinePorath.com accessed August 23, 2017, http://www.christineporath.com/.

2. Corky Siemaszko, "Roger Ailes Scandal: Julie Roginsky Hit Fox News with Sexual Harassment Suit," MSNBC News, April 4, 2017, accessed August 23, 2017, https://www.nbcnews.com/news/us-news/roger-ailes-scandal-embattled-fox-news-hit-another-sex-harassment-n742066.

3. Christina Zdanowicz and Emanuella Grinburg, "Passenger Dragged Off Overbooked United Flight," CNN.com, April 11, 2017, accessed August 23, 2017, http://www.cnn.com/2017/04/10/travel/passenger-removed-united-flight-trnd/index.html.

4. Aly Weisman, "Steven Tyler Blasts Former Manager in $8M Suit for Being Rude and 'Verbally Abusive,'" BusinessInsider.com, December 18, 2012, accessed September 10, 2017, http://www.businessinsider.com/steven-tyler-blasts-former-manager-in-8m-suit-for-being-rude-and-verbally-abusive-2012-12.

CHAPTER 4

1. David L. Cooperider, Diana Whitney, and Jacqueline M. Stavros, *Appreciative Inquiry Handbook, the First in a Series of AI Workbooks for Leaders of Change* (Bedford Heights, OH: Lakeshore Publishers, 2003), 83.

2. Jane Magruder Watkins and Bernard J. Mohr, *Appreciative Inquiry, Change at the Speed of Imagination* (San Francisco: Jossey-Bass/Pfeiffer, 2001), 25.

INDEX

A

B

C

D

E

F

W